HIS OWN PEOPLE

Booth Tarkington

1st WORLD
LIBRARY
Literary Society

His Own People

Booth Tarkington

© 1st World Library – Literary Society, 2005
PO Box 2211
Fairfield, IA 52556
www.1stworldlibrary.org
First Edition

LCCN: 2004195587

Softcover ISBN: 1-4218-0408-5
Hardcover ISBN: 1-4218-0308-9
eBook ISBN: 1-4218-0508-1

Purchase *"His Own People"*
as a traditional bound book at:
www.1stWorldLibrary.org/purchase.asp?ISBN=1-4218-0408-5

1st World Library Literary Society is a nonprofit organization dedicated to promoting literacy by:

- Creating a free internet library accessible from any computer worldwide.
- Hosting writing competitions and offering book publishing scholarships.

Readers interested in supporting literacy through sponsorship, donations or membership please contact:
literacy@1stworldlibrary.org
Check us out at: www.1stworldlibrary.ORG
and start downloading free ebooks today.

His Own People
contributed by Tim, Ed & Rodney
in support of
1st World Library Literary Society

I.

A CHANGE OF LODGING

The glass-domed "palm-room" of the Grand Continental Hotel Magnifique in Rome is of vasty heights and distances, filled with a mellow green light which filters down languidly through the upper foliage of tall palms, so that the two hundred people who may be refreshing or displaying themselves there at the tea-hour have something the look of under-water creatures playing upon the sea-bed. They appear, however, to be unaware of their condition; even the ladies, most like anemones of that gay assembly, do not seem to know it; and when the Hungarian band (crustacean-like in costume, and therefore well within the picture) has sheathed its flying tentacles and withdrawn by dim processes, the tea-drinkers all float out through the doors, instead of bubbling up and away through the filmy roof. In truth, some such exit as that was imagined for them by a young man who remained in the aquarium after they had all gone, late one afternoon of last winter. They had been marvelous enough, and to him could have seemed little more so had they made such a departure. He could almost have gone that way himself, so charged was he with the uplift of his belief that, in spite of the brilliant strangeness of the hour just past, he had been no fish out of water.

While the waiters were clearing the little tables, he leaned back in his chair in a content so rich it was nearer ecstasy. He could not bear to disturb the possession joy had taken of him, and, like a half-awake boy clinging to a dream that his hitherto unkind sweetheart has kissed him, lingered on in the enchanted atmosphere, his eyes still full of all they had beheld with such delight, detaining and smiling upon each revelation of this fresh memory - the flashingly lovely faces, the dreamily lovely faces, the pearls and laces of the anemone ladies, the color and romantic fashion of the uniforms, and the old princes who had been pointed out to him: splendid old men wearing white mustaches and single eye-glasses, as he had so long hoped and dreamed they did.

"Mine own people!" he whispered. "I have come unto mine own at last. Mine own people!" After long waiting (he told himself), he had seen them - the people he had wanted to see, wanted to know, wanted to be *of!* Ever since he had begun to read of the "beau monde" in his schooldays, he had yearned to know some such sumptuous reality as that which had come true to-day, when, at last, in Rome he had seen - as he wrote home that night - "the finest essence of Old-World society mingling in Cosmopolis."

Artificial odors (too heavy to keep up with the crowd that had worn them) still hung about him; he breathed them deeply, his eyes half-closed and his lips noise-lessly formed themselves to a quotation from one of his own poems:

> While trails of scent, like cobweb's films
> Slender and faint and rare,
> Of roses, and rich, fair fabrics,

Cling on the stirless air,
The sibilance of voices,
At a wave of Milady's glove,
Is stilled -

He stopped short, interrupting himself with a half-cough of laughter as he remembered the inspiration of these verses. He had written them three months ago, at home in Cranston, Ohio, the evening after Anna McCord's "coming-out tea." "Milady" meant Mrs. McCord; she had "stilled" the conversation of her guests when Mary Kramer (whom the poem called a "sweet, pale singer") rose to sing Mavourneen; and the stanza closed with the right word to rhyme with "glove." He felt a contemptuous pity for his little, untraveled, provincial self of three months ago, if, indeed, it could have been himself who wrote verses about Anna McCord's "coming-out tea" and referred to poor, good old Mrs. McCord as "Milady"!

The second stanza had intimated a conviction of a kind which only poets may reveal:

She sang to that great assembly,
They thought, as they praised her tone;
But she and my heart knew better:
Her song was for me alone.

He had told the truth when he wrote of Mary Kramer as pale and sweet, and she was paler, but no less sweet, when he came to say good-by to her before he sailed. Her face, as it was at the final moment of the protracted farewell, shone before him very clearly now for a moment: young, plaintive, white, too lamentably honest to conceal how much her "God-speed" to him cost her. He came very near telling her how fond of her he had always been; came near giving up his great trip to remain with her always.

"Ah!" He shivered as one shivers at the thought of disaster narrowly averted. "The fates were good that I only came near it!"

He took from his breast-pocket an engraved card, without having to search for it, because during the few days the card had been in his possession the action had become a habit.

"Comtesse de Vaurigard," was the name engraved, and below was written in pencil: "To remember Monsieur Robert Russ Mellin he promise to come to tea Hotel Magnifique, Roma, at five o'clock Thursday."

There had been disappointment in the first stages of his journey, and that had gone hard with Mellin. Europe had been his goal so long, and his hopes of pleasure grew so high when (after his years of saving and putting by, bit by bit, out of his salary in a real-estate office) he drew actually near the shining horizon. But London, his first stopping-place, had given him some dreadful days. He knew nobody, and had not understood how heavily sheer loneliness - which was something he had never felt until then - would weigh upon his spirits. In Cranston, where the young people "grew up together," and where he met a dozen friends on the street in a half-hour's walk, he often said that he "liked to be alone with himself." London, after his first excitement in merely being there, taught him his mistake, chilled him with weeks of forbidding weather, puzzled and troubled him.

He was on his way to Paris when (as he recorded in his

journal) a light came into his life. This illumination first shone for him by means of one Cooley, son and inheritor of all that had belonged to the late great Cooley, of Cooley Mills, Connecticut. Young Cooley, a person of cheery manners and bright waistcoats, was one of Mellin's few sea-acquaintances; they had played shuffleboard together on the steamer during odd half-hours when Mr. Cooley found it possible to absent himself from poker in the smoking-room; and they encountered each other again on the channel boat crossing to Calais.

"Hey!" was Mr. Cooley's lively greeting. "I'm meetin' lots of people I know to-day. You runnin' over to Paris, too? Come up to the boat-deck and meet the Countess de Vaurigard."

"Who?" said Mellin, red with pleasure, yet fearing that he did not hear aright.

"The Countess de Vaurigard. Queen! met her in London. Sneyd introduced me to her. You remember Sneyd on the steamer? Baldish Englishman - red nose - doesn't talk much - younger brother of Lord Rugden, so he says. Played poker some. Well, *yes!"*

"I saw him. I didn't meet him."

"You didn't miss a whole lot. Fact is, before we landed I almost had him sized up for queer, but when he introduced me to the Countess I saw my mistake. He must be the real thing. *She* certainly is! You come along up and see."

So Mellin followed, to make his bow before a thin, dark, charmingly pretty young woman, who smiled up at him from her deck-chair through an enhancing mystery of veils; and presently he found himself sitting beside her. He could not help trembling slightly at first, but he would have giving a great deal if, by some miraculous vision, Mary Kramer and other friends of his in Cranston could have seen him engaged in what he thought of as "conversational badinage" with the Comtesse de Vaurigard.

Both the lady and her name thrilled him. He thought he remembered the latter in Froissart: it conjured up "baronial halls" and "donjon keeps," rang resonantly in his mind like "Let the portcullis fall!" At home he had been wont to speak of the "oldest families in Cranston," complaining of the invasions of "new people" into the social territory of the McCords and Mellins and Kramers - a pleasant conception which the presence of a De Vaurigard revealed to him as a petty and shameful fiction; and yet his humility, like his little fit of trembling, was of short duration, for gay geniality of Madame de Vaurigard put him amazingly at ease.

At Calais young Cooley (with a matter-of-course air, and not seeming to feel the need of asking permission) accompanied her to a compartment, and Mellin walked with them to the steps of the coach, where he paused, murmuring some words of farewell.

Madame de Vaurigard turned to him with a prettily assumed dismay.

"What! You stay at Calais?" she cried, pausing with one foot on the step to ascend. "Oh! I am sorry for you. Calais is terrible!"

"No. I am going on to Paris."

"So? You have frien's in another coach which you wish to be wiz?"

"No, no, indeed," he stammered hastily.

"Well, my frien'," she laughed gayly, "w'y don' you come wiz us?"

Blushing, he followed Cooley into the coach, to spend five happy hours, utterly oblivious of the bright French landscape whirling by outside the window.

There ensued a month of conscientious sightseeing in Paris, and that unfriendly city afforded him only one glimpse of the Countess. She whizzed by him in a big touring-car one afternoon as he stood on an "isle of safety" at the foot of the Champs Elysees. Cooley was driving the car. The raffish, elderly Englishman (whose name, Mellin knew, was Sneyd) sat with him, and beside Madame de Vaurigard in the tonneau lolled a gross-looking man - unmistakably an American - with a jovial, red, smooth-shaven face and several chins. Brief as the glimpse was, Mellin had time to receive a distinctly disagreeable impression of this person, and to wonder how Heaven could vouchsafe the society of Madame de Vaurigard to so coarse a creature.

All the party were dressed as for the road, gray with dust, and to all appearances in a merry mood. Mellin's heart gave a leap when he saw that the Countess recognized him. Her eyes, shining under a white veil, met his for just the instant before she was quite by, and when the machine had passed a little handkerchief waved for a moment from the side of the tonneau where she sat.

With that he drew the full breath of Romance.

He had always liked to believe that "*grandes dames*" leaned back in the luxurious upholstery of their victorias, landaulettes, daumonts or automobiles with an air of inexpressible though languid hauteur. The Newport letter in the Cranston Telegraph often referred to it. But the gayety of that greeting from the Countess' little handkerchief was infinitely refreshing, and Mellin decided that animation was more becoming than hauteur - even to a *"grande dame."*

That night he wrote (almost without effort) the verses published in the Cranston Telegraph two weeks later. They began:

> *Marquise, ma belle*, with your kerchief of lace
> Awave from your flying car,
> And your slender hand -

The hand to which he referred was the same which had arrested his gondola and his heart simultaneously, five days ago, in Venice. He was on his way to the station when Madame de Vaurigard's gondola shot out into the Grand Canal from a narrow channel, and at her signal both boats paused.

"Ah! but you fly away!" she cried, lifting her eyebrows mournfully, as she saw the steamer-trunk in his gondola. "You are goin' return to America?"

"No. I'm just leaving for Rome."

"Well, in three day' *I* am goin' to Rome!" She clapped

her hands lightly and laughed. "You know this is three time' we meet jus' by chance, though that second time it was so quick - *pff*! like that - we didn't talk much togezzer! Monsieur Mellin," she laughed again, "I think we mus' be frien's. Three time' - an' we are both goin' to Rome! Monsieur Mellin, you believe in *Fate*?"

With a beating heart he did.

Thence came the invitation to meet her at the Magnifique for tea, and the card she scribbled for him with a silver pencil. She gave it with the prettiest gesture, leaning from her gondola to his as they parted. She turned again, as the water between them widened, and with her "*Au revoir*" offered him a faintly wistful smile to remember.

All the way to Rome the noises of the train beat out the measure of his Parisian verses:

Marquise, ma belle, with your kerchief of lace
Awave from your flying car -

He came out of his reverie with a start. A dozen men and women, dressed for dinner, with a gold-fish officer or two among them, swam leisurely through the aquarium on their way to the hotel restaurant. They were the same kind of people who had sat at the little tables for tea - people of the great world, thought Mellin: no vulgar tourists or "trippers" among them; and he shuddered at the remembrance of his pension (whither it was time to return) and its conscientious students of Baedeker, its dingy halls and permanent smell of cold food. Suddenly a high resolve lit his face: he got his coat and hat from the brass-and-blue custodian in the lobby, and without hesitation entered the "bureau."

"I 'm not quite satisfied where I am staying - where I'm stopping, that is," he said to the clerk. "I think I'll take a room here."

"Very well, sir. Where shall I send for your luggage?"

"I shall bring it myself," replied Mellin coldly, "in my cab."

He did not think it necessary to reveal the fact that he was staying at one of the cheaper pensions; and it may be mentioned that this reticence (as well as the somewhat chilling, yet careless, manner of a gentleman of the "great world" which he assumed when he returned with his trunk and bag) very substantially increased the rate put upon the room he selected at the Magnifique. However, it was with great satisfaction that he found himself installed in the hotel, and he was too recklessly exhilarated, by doing what he called the "right thing," to waste any time wondering what the "right thing" would do to the diminishing pad of express checks he carried in the inside pocket of his waistcoat.

"Better live a fortnight like a gentleman," he said, as he tossed his shoes into a buhl cabinet, "than vegetate like a tourist for a year."

He had made his entrance into the "great world" and he meant to hold his place in it as one "to the manor born." Its people should not find him lacking: he would wear their manner and speak their language - no gaucherie should betray him, no homely phrase escape his lips.

This was the chance he had always hoped for, and when he fell asleep in his gorgeous, canopied bed, his soul was uplifted with happy expectations.

II.

MUSIC ON THE PINCIO

The following afternoon found him still in that enviable condition as he stood listening to the music on the Pincian Hill. He had it of rumor that the Fashion of Rome usually took a turn there before it went to tea, and he had it from the lady herself that Madame de Vaurigard would be there. Presently she came, reclining in a victoria, the harness of her horses flashing with gold in the sunshine. She wore a long ermine stole; her hat was ermine; she carried a muff of the same fur, and Mellin thought it a perfect finish to the picture that a dark gentleman of an appearance most distinguished should be sitting beside her. An Italian noble, surely!

He saw the American at once, nodded to him and waved her hand. The victoria went on a little way beyond the turn of the drive, drew out of the line of carriages, and stopped.

"Ah, Monsieur Mellin," she cried, as he came up, "I am glad! I was so foolish yesterday I didn' give you the address of my little apartment an' I forgot to ask you what is your hotel. I tol' you I would come here for my drive, but still I might have lost you for ever. See what many people! It is jus' that Fate again."

She laughed, and looked to the Italian for sympathy in her kindly merriment. He smiled cordially upon her, then lifted his hat and smiled as cordially upon Mellin.

"I am so happy to fin' myself in Rome that I forget" - Madame de Vaurigard went on - "*ever'sing!* But now I mus' make sure not to lose you. What is your hotel?"

"Oh, the Magnifique," Mellin answered carelessly. "I suppose everybody that one knows stops there. One does stop there, when one is in Rome, doesn't one?"

"Everybody go' there for tea, and to eat, sometime, but to *stay* - ah, that is for the American!" she laughed. "That is for you who are all so abomin-*ab*-ly rich!" She smiled to the Italian again, and both of them smiled beamingly on Mellin.

"But that isn't always our fault, is it?" said Mellin easily.

"Aha! You mean you are of the new generation, of the yo'ng American' who come over an' try to spen' these immense fortune' - those *'pile'* - your father or your gran-father make! I know quite well. Ah?"

"Well," he hesitated, smiling. "I suppose it does look a little by way of being like that."

"Wicked fellow!" She leaned forward and tapped his shoulder chidingly with two fingers. "I know what you wish the mos' in the worl' - you wish to get into mischief. That is it! No, sir, I will jus' take you in han'!"

"When will you take me?" he asked boldly.

At this, the pleasant murmur of laughter - half actual and half suggested - with which she underlined the conversation, became loud and clear, as she allowed her vivacious glance to strike straight into his upturned eyes, and answered:

"As long as a little turn roun' the hill, *now*. Cavaliere Corni -"

To Mellin's surprise and delight the Italian immediately descended from the victoria without the slightest appearance of irritation; on the contrary, he was urbane to a fine degree, and, upon Madame de Vaurigard's formally introducing him to Mellin, saluted the latter with grave politeness, expressing in good English a hope that they might meet often. When the American was installed at the Countess' side she spoke to the driver in Italian, and they began to move slowly along the ilex avenue, the coachman reining his horses to a walk.

"You speak Italian?" she inquired.

"Oh, not a great deal more than a smattering," he replied airily - a truthful answer, inasmuch as a vocabulary consisting simply of *"quanty costy"* and *"troppo"* cannot be seriously considered much more than a smattering. Fortunately she made no test of his linguistic attainment, but returned to her former subject.

"Ah, yes, all the worl' to-day know' the new class of American," she said - "*your* class. Many year' ago we have another class which Europe didn' like. That was when the American was ter-ri-ble! He was the - what is that you call? - oh, yes; he 'make himself,' you say: that is it. My frien', he was abominable! He brag'; he talk' through the nose; yes, and he was niggardly, rich as he was! But you, you yo'ng men of the new generation, you are gentlemen of the idleness; you are aristocrats, with polish an' with culture. An' yet you throw your money away - yes, you throw it to poor Europe as if to a beggar!"

"No, no," he protested with an indulgent laugh which confessed that the truth was really "Yes, yes."

"Your smile betray' you!" she cried triumphantly. "More than jus' bein' guilty of that fault, I am goin' to tell you of others. You are not the ole-time - what is it you say? - Ah, yes, the 'goody-goody.' I have heard my great American frien', Honor-able Chanlair Pedlow, call it the Sonday-school. Is it not? Yes, you are not the Sonday-school yo'ng men, you an' your class!"

"No," he said, bestowing a long glance upon a stout nurse who was sitting on a bench near the drive and attending to twins in a perambulator. "No, we're not exactly dissenting parsons."

"Ah, no!" She shook her head at him prettily. "You are wicked! You are up into all the mischief! Have I not hear what wild sums you risk at your game, that poker? You are famous for it."

"Oh, we play," he admitted with a reckless laugh, "and I suppose we do play rather high."

"High!" she echoed. "*Souzands!* But that is not all. Ha, ha, ha, naughty one! Have I not observe' you lookin' at these pretty creature', the little contadina-girl, an' the poor ladies who have hire' their carriages for two lire to drive up and down the Pincio in their bes' dress an' be admire' by the yo'ng American while the music play'? Which one I wonder, is it on whose wrist you would mos' like to fasten a bracelet of diamon's? Wicked, I have watch' you look at them -"

"No, no," he interrupted earnestly. "I have not once looked away from you, I *could n't*." Their eyes met, but instantly hers were lowered; the bright smile with which she had been rallying him faded and there was a pause during which he felt that she had become very grave. When she spoke, it was with a little quaver, and the controlled pathos of her voice was so intense that it evoked a sympathetic catch in his own throat.

"But, my frien', if it should be that I cannot wish you to look so at me, or to speak so to me?"

"I beg your pardon!" he exclaimed, almost incoherently. "I didn't mean to hurt your feelings. I wouldn't do anything you'd think ungentlemanly for the world!"

Her eyes lifted again to his with what he had no difficulty in recognizing as a look of perfect trust; but, behind that, he perceived a darkling sadness.

"I know it is true," she murmured - "I know. But you see there are time' when a woman has sorrow - sorrow of one kind - when she mus' be sure that there is only - only rispec' in the hearts of her frien's."

With that, the intended revelation was complete, and the young man understood, as clearly as if she had told him in so many words, that she was not a widow and that her husband was the cause of her sorrow. His quickened instinct marvelously divined (or else it was

Booth Tarkington

conveyed to him by some intangible method of hers) that the Count de Vaurigard was a very bad case, but that she would not divorce him.

"I know," he answered, profoundly touched. "I understand."

In silent gratitude she laid her hand for a second upon his sleeve. Then her face brightened, and she said gayly:

"But we shall not talk of *me!* Let us see how we can keep you out of mischief at leas' for a little while. I know very well what you will do to-night: you will go to Salone Margherita an' sit in a box like all the wicked Americans -"

"No, indeed, I shall not!"

"Ah, yes, you will!" she laughed. "But until dinner let me keep you from wickedness. Come to tea jus' wiz me, not at the hotel, but at the little apartment I have taken, where it is quiet. The music is finish', an' all those pretty girl' are goin' away, you see. I am not selfish if I take you from the Pincio now. You will come?

III.

GLAMOUR

It was some fair dream that would be gone too soon, he told himself, as they drove rapidly through the twilight streets, down from the Pincio and up the long slope of the Quirinal. They came to a stop in the gray courtyard of a palazzo, and ascended in a sleepy elevator to the fifth floor. Emerging, they encountered a tall man who was turning away from the Countess' door, which he had just closed. The landing was not lighted, and for a moment he failed to see the American following Madame de Vaurigard.

"Eow, it's you, is it," he said informally. "Waitin' a devil of a long time for you. I've gawt a message for you. *He's* comin'. He writes that Cooley -"

"Attention!" she interrupted under her breath, and, stepping forward quickly, touched the bell. "I have brought a frien' of our dear, droll Cooley with me to tea. Monsieur Mellin, you mus' make acquaintance with Monsieur Sneyd. He is English, but we shall forgive him because he is a such ole frien' of mine."

"Ah, yes," said Mellin. "Remember seeing you on the boat, running across the pond."

"Yes, ev coss," responded Mr. Sneyd cordially. "I wawsn't so fawchnit as to meet you, but dyuh eold Cooley's talked ev you often. Heop I sh'll see maw of you hyuh."

A very trim, very intelligent-looking maid opened the door, and the two men followed Madame de Vaurigard into a square hall, hung with tapestries and lit by two candles of a Brobdingnagian species Mellin had heretofore seen only in cathedrals. Here Mr. Sneyd paused.

"I weon't be bawthring you," he said. "Just a wad with you, Cantess, and I'm off."

The intelligent-looking maid drew back some heavy curtains leading to a salon beyond the hall, and her mistress smiled brightly at Mellin.

"I shall keep him to jus' his one word," she said, as the young man passed between the curtains.

It was a nobly proportioned room that he entered, so large that, in spite of the amount of old furniture it contained, the first impression it gave was one of spaciousness. Panels of carved and blackened wood lined the walls higher than his head; above them, Spanish leather gleamed here and there with flickerings of red and gilt, reflecting dimly a small but brisk wood fire which crackled in a carved stone fireplace. His feet slipped on the floor of polished tiles and wandered from silky rugs to lose themselves in great black bear skins as in unmown sward. He went from the portrait of a "cinquecento" cardinal to a splendid tryptich set over a Gothic chest, from a cabinet sheltering a collection of old glass to an Annunciation by an unknown Primitive. He told himself that this was a "room in a book," and became dreamily assured that he was a man in a book. Finally he stumbled upon something almost grotesquely out of place: a large, new, perfectly-appointed card-table with a sliding top, a smooth, thick, green cover and patent compartments.

He halted before this incongruity, regarding it with astonishment. Then a light laugh rippled behind him, and he turned to find Madame de Vaurigard seated in a big red Venetian chair by the fire.

She wore a black lace dress, almost severe in fashion, which gracefully emphasized her slenderness; and she sat with her knees crossed, the firelight twinkling on the beads of her slipper, on her silken instep, and flashing again from the rings upon the slender fingers she had clasped about her knee.

She had lit a thin, long Russian cigarette.

"You see?" she laughed. "I mus' keep up with the time. I mus' do somesing to hold my frien's about me. Even the ladies like to play now - that breedge w'ich is so tiresome - they play, play, play! And you - you Americans, you refuse to endure us if we do not let you play. So for my frien's when they come to my house - if they wish it, there is that foolish little table. I fear" - she concluded with a bewitching affectation of sadness - "they prefer that to talkin' wiz me."

"You know that couldn't be so, *Comtesse*," he said. "I would rather talk to you than - than -"

"Ah, yes, you say so, Monsieur!" She looked at him gravely; a little sigh seemed to breathe upon her lips;

she leaned forward nearer the fire, her face wistful in the thin, rosy light, and it seemed to him he had never seen anything so beautiful in his life.

He came across to her and sat upon a stool at her feet. "On my soul," he began huskily, "I swear -"

She laid her finger on her lips, shaking her head gently; and he was silent, while the intelligent maid - at that moment entering - arranged a tea-table and departed.

"American an' Russian, they are the worse," said the Countess thoughtfully, as she served him with a generous cup, laced with rum, "but the American he is the bes' to play *wiz.*" Mellin found her irresistible when she said "wiz."

"Why is that?"

"Oh, the Russian play high, yes - but the American" - she laughed delightedly and stretched her arms wide - "he make' it all a joke! He is beeg like his beeg country. If he win or lose, he don' care! Ah, I mus' tell you of my great American frien', that Honor-able Chanlair Pedlow, who is comin' to Rome. You have heard of Honor-able Chanlair Pedlow in America?"

"I remember hearing that name."

"Ah, I shall make you know him. He is a man of distinction; he did sit in your Chamber of Deputies - what you call it? - yes, your Con-gress. He is funny, eccentric - always he roar like a lion - Boum! - but so simple, so good, a man of such fine heart - so lovable!"

"1'll be glad to meet him," said Mellin coldly.

"An', oh, yes, I almos' forget to tell you," she went on, "your frien', that dear Cooley, he is on his way from Monte Carlo in his automobile. I have a note from him to-day."

"Good sort of fellow, little Cooley, in his way," remarked her companion graciously. "Not especially intellectual or that, you know. His father was a manufacturer chap, I believe, or something of the sort. I suppose you saw a lot of him in Paris?"

"Eh, I thought he is dead!" cried Madame de Vaurigard.

"The father is. I mean, little Cooley."

"Oh, yes," she laughed softly. "We had some gay times, a little party of us. We shall be happy here, too; you will see. I mus' make a little dinner very soon, but not unless you will come. You will?"

"Do you want me very much?"

He placed his empty cup on the table and leaned closer to her, smiling. She did not smile in response; instead, her eyes fell and there was the faintest, pathetic quiver of her lower lip.

"Already you know that," she said in a low voice.

She rose quickly, turned away from him and walked across the room to the curtains which opened upon the hall. One of these she drew back.

"My frien', you mus' go now," she said in the same low voice. "To-morrow I will see you again. Come at four an' you shall drive with me - but not - not more - *now*. Please!"

She stood waiting, not looking at him, but with head bent and eyes veiled. As he came near she put out a limp hand. He held it for a few seconds of distinctly emotional silence, then strode swiftly into the hall.

She immediately let the curtain fall behind him, and as he got his hat and coat he heard her catch her breath sharply with a sound like a little sob.

Dazed with glory, he returned to the hotel. In the lobby he approached the glittering concierge and said firmly:

"What is the Salone Margherita? Cam you get me a box there to-night?"

IV.

GOOD FELLOWSHIP

He confessed his wickedness to Madame de Vaurigard the next afternoon as they drove out the Appian Way. "A fellow must have just a bit of a fling, you know," he said; "and, really, Salone Margherita isn't so tremendously wicked."

She shook her head at him in friendly raillery. "Ah, that may be; but how many of those little dancing-girl' have you invite to supper afterward?"

This was a delicious accusation, and though he shook his head in virtuous denial he was before long almost convinced that he *had* given a rather dashing supper after the vaudeville and had *not* gone quietly back to the hotel, only stopping by the way to purchase an orange and a pocketful of horse-chestnuts to eat in his room.

It was a happy drive for Robert Russ Mellin, though not happier than that of the next day. Three afternoons they spent driving over the Campagna, then back to Madame de Vaurigard's apartment for tea by the firelight, till the enraptured American began to feel that the dream in which he had come to live must of happy necessity last forever.

On the fourth afternoon, as he stepped out of the hotel elevator into the corridor, he encountered Mr. Sneyd.

"Just stottin', eh?" said the Englishman, taking an envelope from his pocket. "Lucky I caught you. This is for you. I just saw the Cantess and she teold me to give it you. Herry and read it and kem on t' the Amairikin Baw. Chap I want you to meet. Eold Cooley's thyah too. Gawt in with his tourin'-caw at noon."

"You will forgive, dear friend," wrote Madame de Vaurigard, "if I ask you that we renounce our drive to-day. You see, I wish to have that little dinner to-night and must make preparation. Honorable Chandler Pedlow arrived this morning from Paris and that droll Mr. Cooley I have learn is coincidentally arrived also. You see I think it would be very pleasant to have the dinner to welcome these friends on their arrival. You will come surely - or I shall be so truly miserable. You know it perhaps too well! We shall have a happy evening if you come to console us for renouncing our drive. A thousand of my prettiest wishes for you.

"Helene."

The signature alone consoled him. To have that note from her, to own it, was like having one of her gloves or her fan. He would keep it forever, he thought; indeed, he more than half expressed a sentiment to that effect in the response which he wrote in the aquarium, while Sneyd waited for him at a table near by. The Englishman drew certain conclusions in regard to this reply, since it permitted a waiting friend to consume three long tumblers of brandy-and-soda before it was finished. However, Mr. Sneyd kept his reflections to himself, and, when the epistle had been dispatched by a messenger, took the American's arm and led him to the "American Bar" of the hotel, a region hitherto unexplored by Mellin.

Leaning against the bar were Cooley and the man whom Mellin had seen lolling beside Madame de Vaurigard in Cooley's automobile in Paris, the same gross person for whom he had instantly conceived a strong repugnance, a feeling not at once altered by a closer view.

Cooley greeted Mellin uproariously and Mr. Sneyd introduced the fat man. "Mr. Mellin, the Honorable Chandler Pedlow," he said; nor was the shock to the first-named gentleman lessened by young Cooley's adding, "Best feller in the world!"

Mr. Pedlow's eyes were sheltered so deeply beneath florid rolls of flesh that all one saw of them was an inscrutable gleam of blue; but, small though they were, they were not shifty, for they met Mellin's with a squareness that was almost brutal. He offered a fat paw, wet by a full glass which he set down too suddenly on the bar.

"Shake," he said, in a loud and husky voice, "and be friends! Tommy," he added to the attendant, "another round of Martinis."

"Not for me," said Mellin hastily. "I don't often -"

"*What!*" Mr. Pedlow roared suddenly. "Why, the first words Countess de Vaurigard says to me this afternoon was, 'I want you to meet my young friend Mellin,' she says; 'the gamest little Indian that ever come down the pike! He's game,' she says - 'he'll see you *all* under the table!' That's what the smartest little woman in the world, the Countess de Vaurigard, says about you."

This did not seem very closely to echo Madame de Vaurigard's habit of phrasing, but Mellin perceived that it might be only the fat man's way of putting things.

"You ain't goin' back on *her*, are you?" continued Mr. Pedlow. "You ain't goin' to make her out a liar? I tell you, when the Countess de Vaurigard says a man 's game, he is game!" He laid his big paw cordially on Mellin's shoulder and smiled, lowering his voice to a friendly whisper. "And I'll bet ten thousand dollars right out of my pants pocket you *are* game, too!"

He pressed a glass into the other's hand. Smiling feebly, the embarrassed Mellin accepted it.

"Make it four more, Tommy," said Pedlow. "And here," continued this thoughtful man, "I don't go bandying no ladies' names around a bar-room - that ain't my style - but I do want to propose a toast. I won't name her, but you all know who I mean."

"Sure we do," interjected Cooley warmly. "Queen! That's what she is."

"Here's *to* her," continued Mr. Pedlow. "Here's to her - brightest and best - and no heel-taps! And now let's set down over in the corner and take it easy. It ain't hardly five o'clock yet, and we can set here comfortable, gittin' ready for dinner, until half-past six, anyway."

Whereupon the four seated themselves about a tabouret

in the corner, and, a waiter immediately bringing them four fresh glasses from the bar, Mellin began to understand what Mr. Pedlow meant by "gittin' ready for dinner." The burden of the conversation was carried almost entirely by the Honorable Chandler, though Cooley, whose boyish face was deeply flushed, now and then managed to interrupt by talking louder than the fat man. Mr. Sneyd sat silent.

"Good ole Sneyd," said Pedlow. "~He~ never talks, jest saws wood. Only Britisher I ever liked. Plays cards like a goat."

"He played a mighty good game on the steamer," said Cooley warmly.

"I don't care what he did on the steamer, he played like a goat the only time *I* ever played with him. You know he did. I reckon you was *there!*"

"Should say I *was* there! He played mighty well -"

"Like a goat," reiterated the fat man firmly.

"Nothing of the sort. You had a run of hands, that was all. Nobody can go against the kind of luck you had that night; and you took it away from Sneyd and me in rolls. But we'll land you pretty soon, won't we, ole Sneydie?"

"We sh'll have a shawt at him, at least," said the Englishman.

"Perhaps he won't want us to try," young Cooley pursued derisively. "Perhaps he thinks I play like a goat, too!"

Mr. Pedlow threw back his head and roared. "Give me somep'n easy! You don't know no more how to play a hand of cards than a giraffe does. I'll throw in all of my Blue Gulch gold-stock - and it's worth eight hundred thousand dollars if it's worth a cent - I'll put it up against that tin automobile of yours, divide chips even and play you freeze-out for it. You play cards? Go learn hop-scotch!"

"You wait!" exclaimed the other indignantly. "Next time we play we'll make you look so small you'll think you're back in Congress!"

At this Mr. Pedlow again threw back his head and roared, his vast body so shaken with mirth that the glass he held in his hand dropped to the floor.

"There," said Cooley, "that's the second Martini you've spilled. You're two behind the rest of us."

"What of it?" bellowed the fat man. "There's plenty comin', ain't there? Four more, Tommy, and bring cigars. Don't take a cent from none of these Indians. Gentlemen, your money ain't good here. I own this bar, and this is my night."

Mellin had begun to feel at ease, and after a time - as they continued to sit - he realized that his repugnance to Mr. Pedlow was wearing off; he felt that there must be good in any one whom Madame de Vaurigard liked. She had spoken of Pedlow often on their drives; he was an "eccentric," she said, an "original." Why not accept her verdict? Besides, Pedlow was a man of distinction and force; he had been in Congress; he was a millionaire; and, as became evident in the course of a long recital of the principal events of his career, most of the great men of the time were his friends and proteges.

"'Well, Mack,' says I one day when we were in the House together" - (thus Mr. Pedlow, alluding to the late President McKinley) - "'Mack,' says I, 'if you'd drop that double standard business' - he was waverin' toward silver along then - 'I don't know but I might git the boys to nominate you fer President.' 'I'll think it over,' he says - 'I'll think it over.' You remember me tellin' you about that at the time, don't you, Sneyd, when you was in the British Legation at Washin'ton?"

"Pahfictly," said Mr. Sneyd, lighting a cigar with great calmness.

"'Yes,' I says, 'Mack,' I says, "if you'll drop it, I'll turn in and git you the nomination.'"

"Did he drop it?" asked Mellin innocently.

Mr. Pedlow leaned forward and struck the young man's knee a resounding blow with the palm of his hand.

"He was *nominated*, wasn't he?"

"Time to dress," announced Mr. Sneyd, looking at his watch.

"One more round first," insisted Cooley with prompt vehemence. "Let's finish with our first toast again. Can't drink that too often."

This proposition was received with warmest approval, and they drank standing. "Brightest and best!" shouted Mr. Pedlow.

"Queen! What she is!" exclaimed Cooley.

"Ma belle Marquise!" whispered Mellin tenderly, as the rim touched his lips.

A small, keen-faced man, whose steady gray eyes were shielded by tortoise-rimmed spectacles, had come into the room and now stood quietly at the bar, sipping a glass of Vichy. He was sharply observant of the party as it broke up, Pedlow and Sneyd preceding the younger men to the corridor, and, as the latter turned to follow, the stranger stepped quickly forward, speaking Cooley's name.

"What's the matter?"

"Perhaps you don't remember me. My name's Cornish. I'm a newspaper man, a correspondent." (He named a New York paper.) "I'm down here to get a Vatican story. I knew your father for a number of years before his death, and I think I may claim that he was a friend of mine."

"That's good," said the youth cordially. "If I hadn't a fine start already, and wasn't in a hurry to dress, we'd have another."

"You were pointed out to me in Paris," continued Cornish. "I found where you were staying and called on you the next day, but you had just started for the Riviera." He hesitated, glancing at Mellin. "Can you give me half a dozen words with you in private?"

"You'll have to excuse me, I'm afraid. I've only got about ten minutes to dress. See you to-morrow."

"I should like it to be as soon as possible," the journalist said seriously. "It isn't on my own account, and I -"

"All right. You come to my room at ten t'morrow morning?"

"Well, if you can't possibly make it to-night," said Cornish reluctantly. "I wish -"

"Can't possibly."

And Cooley, taking Mellin by the arm, walked rapidly down the corridor. "Funny ole correspondent," he murmured. "What do *I* know about the Vatican?"

V.

LADY MOUNT RHYSWICKE

The four friends of Madame de Vaurigard were borne to her apartment from the Magnifique in Cooley's big car. They sailed triumphantly down and up the hills in a cool and bracing air, under a moon that shone as brightly for them as it had for Caesar, and Mellin's soul was buoyant within him. He thought of Cranston and laughed aloud. What would Cranston say if it could see him in a sixty-horse touring-car, with two millionaires and an English diplomat, brother of an earl, and all on the way to dine with a countess? If Mary Kramer could see him!... Poor Mary Kramer! Poor little Mary Kramer!

A man-servant took their coats in Madame de Vaurigard's hall, where they could hear through the curtains the sound of one or two voices in cheerful conversation.

Sneyd held up his hand.

"Listen," he said. "Shawly, that isn't Lady Mount-Rhyswicke's voice! She couldn't be in Reom - always a Rhyswicke Caws'l for Decembah. By Jev, it is!"

"Nothin' of the kind," said Pedlow. "I know Lady

Mount-Rhyswicke as well as I know you. I started her father in business when he was clerkin' behind a counter in Liverpool. I give him the money to begin on. 'Make good,' says I, 'that's all. Make good!' And he done it, too. Educated his daughter fit fer a princess, married her to Mount-Rhyswicke, and when he died left her ten million dollars if he left her a cent! I know Madge Mount-Rhyswicke and that ain't her voice."

A peal of silvery laughter rang from the other side of the curtain.

"They've heard you," said Cooley.

"An' who could help it?" Madame de Vaurigard herself threw back the curtains. "Who could help hear our great, dear, ole lion? How he roar'!"

She wore a white velvet "princesse" gown of a fashion which was a shade less than what is called "daring," with a rope of pearls falling from her neck and a diamond star in her dark hair. Standing with one arm uplifted to the curtains, and with the mellow glow of candles and firelight behind her, she was so lovely that both Mellin and Cooley stood breathlessly still until she changed her attitude. This she did only to move toward them, extending a hand to each, letting Cooley seize the right and Mellin the left.

Each of them was pleased with what he got, particularly Mellin. "The left is nearer the heart," he thought.

She led them through the curtains, not withdrawing her hands until they entered the salon. She might have led them out of her fifth-story window in that fashion, had she chosen.

"My two wicked boys!" she laughed tenderly. This also pleased both of them, though each would have preferred to be her only wicked boy - a preference which, perhaps, had something to do with the later events of the evening.

"Aha! I know you both; before twenty minute' you will be makin' love to Lady Mount-Rhyswicke. Behol' those two already! An' they are only ole frien's."

She pointed to Pedlow and Sneyd. The fat man was shouting at a woman in pink satin, who lounged, half-reclining, among a pile of cushions upon a divan near the fire; Sneyd gallantly bending over her to kiss her hand.

"It is a very little dinner, you see," continued the hostess, "only seven, but we shall be seven time' happier."

The seventh person proved to be the Italian, Corni, who had surrendered his seat in Madame de Vaurigard's victoria to Mellin on the Pincio. He presently made his appearance followed by a waiter bearing a tray of glasses filled with a pink liquid, while the Countess led her two wicked boys across the room to present them to Lady Mount-Rhyswicke. Already Mellin was forming sentences for his next letter to the Cranston Telegraph: "Lady Mount-Rhyswicke said to me the other evening, while discussing the foreign policy of Great Britain, in Comtesse de Vaurigard's salon..." "An English peeress of pronounced literary acumen has been giving me rather confidentially her opinion of our American poets..."

The inspiration of these promising fragments was a large, weary-looking person, with no lack of powdered shoulder above her pink bodice and a profusion of "undulated" hair of so decided a blond that it might have been suspected that the decision had lain with the lady herself.

"Howjdo," she said languidly, when Mellin's name was pronounced to her. "There's a man behind you tryin' to give you something to drink."

"Who was it said these were Martinis?" snorted Pedlow. "They've got perfumery in 'em."

"Ah, what a bad lion it is!" Madame de Vaurigard lifted both hands in mock horror. "Roar, lion, roar!" she cried. "An' think of the emotion of our good Cavaliere Corni, who have come an hour early jus' to make them for us! I ask Monsieur Mellin if it is not good."

"And I'll leave it to Cooley," said Pedlow. "If he can drink all of his I'll eat crow!"

Thus challenged, the two young men smilingly accepted glasses from the waiter, and lifted them on high.

"Same toast," said Cooley. "Queen!"

"A la belle Marquise!"

Gallantly they drained the glasses at a gulp, and Madame de Vaurigard clapped her hands.

"Bravo!" she cried. "You see? Corni and I, we win."

"Look at their faces!" said Mr. Pedlow, tactlessly drawing attention to what was, for the moment, an undeniably painful sight. "Don't tell me an Italian knows how to make a good Martini!"

Mellin profoundly agreed, but, as he joined the small procession to the Countess' dinner-table, he was certain that an Italian at least knew how to make a strong one.

The light in the dining-room was provided by six heavily-shaded candles on the table; the latter decorated with delicate lines of orchids. The chairs were large and comfortable, covered with tapestry; the glass was old Venetian, and the servants, moving like useful ghosts in the shadow outside the circle of mellow light, were particularly efficient in the matter of keeping the wine-glasses full. Madame de Vaurigard had put Pedlow on her right, Cooley on her left, with Mellin directly opposite her, next to Lady Mount-Rhyswicke. Mellin was pleased, because he thought he would have the Countess's face toward him. Anything would have pleased him just then.

"This is the kind of table *everybody* ought to have," he observed to the party in general, as he finished his first glass of champagne. "I'm going to have it like this at my place in the States - if I ever decide to go back. I'll have six separate candlesticks like this, not a candelabrum, and that will be the only light in the room. And I'll never have anything but orchids on my table -"

"For my part," Lady Mount-Rhyswicke interrupted in the loud, tired monotone which seemed to be her only manner of speaking, "I like more light. I like all the light that's goin'."

"If Lady Mount-Rhyswicke sat at *my* table," returned Mellin dashingly, "I should wish all the light in the world to shine upon so happy an event."

"Hear the man!" she drawled. "He's proposing to me. Thinks I'm a widow."

There was a chorus of laughter, over which rose the bellow of Mr. Pedlow.

"'He's game!' she says - and *ain't* he?"

Across the table Madame de Vaurigard's eyes met Mellin's with a mocking intelligence so complete that he caught her message without need of the words she noiselessly formed with her lips: "I tol' you you would be making love to her!"

He laughed joyously in answer. Why shouldn't he flirt with Lady Mount-Rhyswicke? He was thoroughly happy; his Helene, his *belle Marquise*, sat across the table from him sending messages to him with her eyes. He adored her, but he liked Lady Mount-Rhyswicke - he liked everybody and everything in the world. He liked Pedlow particularly, and it no longer troubled him that the fat man should be a friend of Madame de Vaurigard. Pedlow was a "character" and a wit as well. Mellin laughed heartily at everything the Honorable Chandler Pedlow said.

"This is life," remarked the young man to his fair neighbor.

"What is? Sittin' round a table, eatin' and drinkin'?"

"Ah, lovely skeptic!" She looked at him strangely, but

he continued with growing enthusiasm: "I mean to sit at such a table as this, with such a chef, with such wines - to know one crowded hour like this is to live! Not a thing is missing; all this swagger furniture, the rich atmosphere of smartness about the whole place; best of all, the company. It's a great thing to have the *real* people around you, the right sort, you know, socially; people you'd ask to your own table at home. There are only seven, but every one *distingue*, every one -"

She leaned both elbows on the table with her hands palm to palm, and, resting her cheek against the back of her left hand, looked at him steadily.

"And you - are you distinguished, too?"

"Oh, I wouldn't be much known over *here*," he said modestly.

"Do you write poetry?"

"Oh, not professionally, though it is published. I suppose" - he sipped his champagne with his head a little to one side as though judging its quality - "I suppose I 've been more or less a dilettante. I've knocked about the world a good bit."

"Helene says you're one of these leisure American billionaires like Mr. Cooley there," she said in her tired voice.

"Oh, none of us are really quite billionaires." He laughed deprecatingly.

"No, I suppose not - not really. Go on and tell me some

more about life and this distinguished company."

"Hey, folks!" Mr. Pedlow's roar broke in upon this dialogue. "You two are gittin' mighty thick over there. We're drinking a toast, and you'll have to break away long enough to join in."

"Queen! That's what she is!" shouted Cooley.

Mellin lifted his glass with the others and drank to Madame de Vaurigard, but the woman at his side did not change her attitude and continued to sit with her elbows on the table, her cheek on the back of her hand, watching him thoughtfully.

VI.

RAKE'S PROGRESS

Many toasts were uproariously honored, the health of each member of the party in turn, then the country of each: France and England first, out of courtesy to the ladies, Italy next, since this beautiful and extraordinary meeting of distinguished people (as Mellin remarked in a short speech he felt called upon to make) took place in that wonderful land, then the United States. This last toast the gentlemen felt it necessary to honor by standing in their chairs.

[Song: The Star-Spangled Banner - without words - by Mr. Cooley and chorus.]

When the cigars were brought, the ladies graciously remained, adding tiny spirals of smoke from their cigarettes to the layers of blue haze which soon overhung the table. Through this haze, in the gentle light (which seemed to grow softer and softer) Mellin saw the face of Helene de Vaurigard, luminous as an angel's. She *was* an angel - and the others were gods. What could be more appropriate in Rome? Lady Mount-Rhyswicke was Juno, but more beautiful. For himself, he felt like a god too, Olympic in serenity.

He longed for mysterious dangers. How debonair he

would stroll among them! He wished to explore the unknown; felt the need of a splendid adventure, and had a happy premonition that one was coming nearer and nearer. He favored himself with a hopeful vision of the apartment on fire, Robert Russ Mellin smiling negligently among the flames and Madame de Vaurigard kneeling before him in adoration. Immersed in delight, he puffed his cigar and let his eyes rest dreamily upon the face of Helene. He was quite undisturbed by an argument, more a commotion than a debate, between Mr. Pedlow and young Cooley. It ended by their rising, the latter overturning a chair in his haste.

"I don't know the rudiments, don't I!" cried the boy. "You wait! Ole Sneydie and I'll trim you down! Corni says he'll play, too. Come on, Mellin."

"I won't go unless Helene goes," said Mellin. "What are you going to do when you get there?"

"Alas, my frien'!" exclaimed Madame de Vaurigard, rising, "is it not what I tol' you? Always you are never content wizout your play. You come to dinner an' when it is finish' you play, play, play!"

"*Play*?" He sprang to his feet. "Bravo! That's the very thing I've been wanting to do. I knew there was something I wanted to do, but I couldn't think what it was."

Lady Mount-Rhyswicke followed the others into the salon, but Madame de Vaurigard waited just inside the doorway for Mellin.

"*High* play!" he cried. "We must play high! I won't

play any other way. - I want to play *high*!"

"Ah, wicked one! What did I tell you?"

He caught her hand. "And you must play too, Helene."

"No, no," she laughed breathlessly.

"Then you'll watch. Promise you'll watch me. I won't let you go till you promise to watch me."

"I shall adore it, my frien'!"

"Mellin," called Cooley from the other room. "You comin' or not?"

"Can't you see me?" answered Mellin hilariously, entering with Madame de Vaurigard, who was rosy with laughter. "Peculiar thing to look at a man and not see him."

Candles were lit in many sconces on the walls, and the card-table had been pushed to the centre of the room, little towers of blue, white and scarlet counters arranged upon it in orderly rows like miniature castles.

"Now, then," demanded Cooley, "are the ladies goin' to play?"

"Never!" cried Madame de Vaurigard.

"All right," said the youth cheerfully; "you can look on. Come and sit by me for a mascot."

"You'll need a mascot, my boy!" shouted Pedlow. "That's right, though; take her."

He pushed a chair close to that in which Cooley had already seated himself, and Madame de Vaurigard dropped into it, laughing. "Mellin, you set there," he continued, pushing the young man into a seat opposite Cooley. "We'll give both you young fellers a mascot." He turned to Lady Mount-Rhyswicke, who had gone to the settee by the fire. "Madge, you come and set by Mellin," he commanded jovially. "Maybe he'll forget you ain't a widow again."

"I don't believe I care much about bein' anybody's mascot to-night," she answered. There was a hint of anger in her tired monotone.

"What?" He turned from the table and walked over to the fireplace. "I reckon I didn't understand you," he said quietly, almost gently. "You better come, hadn't you?"

She met his inscrutable little eyes steadily. A faint redness slowly revealed itself on her powdered cheeks; then she followed him back to the table and took the place he had assigned to her at Mellin's elbow.

"I'll bank," said Pedlow, taking a chair between Cooley and the Italian, "unless somebody wants to take it off my hands. Now, what are we playing?"

"Pokah," responded Sneyd with mild sarcasm.

"Bravo!" cried Mellin. "That's *my* game. Ber-*ravo!*"

This was so far true: it was the only game upon which he had ever ventured money; he had played several times when the wagers were allowed to reach a limit of twenty-five cents.

"You know what I mean, I reckon," said Pedlow. "I mean what we are playin' *fer*?"

"Twenty-five franc limit," responded Cooley authoritatively. "Double for jacks. Play two hours and settle when we quit."

Mellin leaned back in his chair. "You call that high?" he asked, with a sniff of contempt. "Why not double it?"

The fat man hammered the table with his fist delightedly. "'He's game,' she says. 'He's the gamest little Indian ever come down the big road!' she says. Was she right? What? Maybe she wasn't! We'll double it before very long, my boy; this'll do to start on. There." He distributed some of the small towers of ivory counters and made a memorandum in a notebook. "There's four hundred apiece."

"That all?" inquired Mellin, whereupon Mr. Pedlow uproariously repeated Madame de Vaurigard's alleged tribute.

As the game began, the intelligent-looking maid appeared from the dining-room, bearing bottles of whisky and soda, and these she deposited upon small tables at the convenience of the players, so that at the conclusion of the first encounter in the gentle tournament there was material for a toast to the gallant who had won it.

"Here's to the gamest Indian of us all," proposed the fat man. "Did you notice him call me with a pair of tens? And me queen-high!"

Mellin drained a deep glass in honor of himself. "On my soul, Chan' Pedlow, I think you're the bes' fellow in the whole world," he said gratefully. "Only trouble with you - you don't want to play high enough."

He won again and again, adding other towers of counters to his original allotment, so that he had the semblance of a tiny castle. When the cards had been dealt for the fifth time he felt the light contact of a slipper touching his foot under the table.

That slipper, he decided (from the nature of things) could belong to none other than his Helene, and even as he came to this conclusion the slight pressure against his foot was gently but distinctly increased thrice. He pressed the slipper in return with his shoe, at the same time giving Madame de Vaurigard a look of grateful surprise and tenderness, which threw her into a confusion so evidently genuine that for an unworthy moment he had a jealous suspicion she had meant the little caress for some other.

It was a disagreeable thought, and, in the hope of banishing it, he refilled his glass; but his mood had begun to change. It seemed to him that Helene was watching Cooley a great deal too devotedly. Why had she consented to sit by Cooley, when she had promised to watch Robert Russ Mellin? He observed the pair stealthily.

Cooley consulted her in laughing whispers upon every discard, upon every bet. Now and then, in their whisperings, Cooley's hair touched hers; sometimes she laid her hand on his the more conveniently to look at his cards. Mellin began to be enraged. Did she think that puling milksop had as much as a shadow of the daring, the devilry, the carelessness of consequences which lay within Robert Russ Mellin? "Consequences?" What were they? There were no such things! She would not look at him - well, he would make her! Thenceforward he raised every bet by another to the extent of the limit agreed upon.

Mr. Cooley was thoroughly happy. He did not resemble Ulysses; he would never have had himself bound to the mast; and there were already sounds of unearthly sweetness in his ears. His conferences with his lovely hostess easily consoled him for his losses. In addition, he was triumphing over the boaster, for Mr. Pedlow, with a very ill grace and swearing (not under his breath), was losing too. The Countess, reiterating for the hundredth time that Cooley was a "wicked one," sweetly constituted herself his cup-bearer; kept his glass full and brought him fresh cigars.

Mellin dealt her furious glances, and filled his own glass, for Lady Mount-Rhyswicke plainly had no conception of herself in the role of a Hebe. The hospitable Pedlow, observing this neglect, was moved to chide her.

"Look at them two cooing doves over there," he said reproachfully, a jerk of his bulbous thumb indicating Madame de Vaurigard and her young protege. "Madge, can't you do nothin' fer our friend the Indian? Can't you even help him to sody?"

"Oh, perhaps," she answered with the slightest flash from her tired eyes. Then she nonchalantly lifted Mellin's replenished glass from the table and drained it. This amused Cooley.

"I like that!" he chuckled. "That's one way of helpin' a feller! Helene, can you do any better than that?"

"Ah, this dear, droll Cooley!"

The tantalizing witch lifted the youth's glass to his lips and let him drink, as a mother helps a thirsty child. "*Bebe!*" she laughed endearingly.

As the lovely Helene pronounced that word, Lady Mount-Rhyswicke was leaning forward to replace Mellin's empty glass upon the table.

"I don't care whether you're a widow or not!" he shouted furiously. And he resoundingly kissed her massive shoulder.

There was a wild shout of laughter; even the imperturbable Sneyd (who had continued to win steadily) wiped tears from his eyes, and Madame de Vaurigard gave way to intermittent hysteria throughout the ensuing half-hour.

For a time Mellin sat grimly observing this inexplicable merriment with a cold smile.

"Laugh on!" he commanded with bitter satire, some ten minutes after play had been resumed - and was instantly obeyed.

Whereupon his mood underwent another change, and he became convinced that the world was a warm and kindly place, where it was good to live. He forgot that he was jealous of Cooley and angry with the Countess; he liked everybody again, especially Lady Mount-Rhyswicke. "Won't you sit farther forward?" he begged her earnestly; "so that I can see your beautiful golden hair?"

He heard but dimly the spasmodic uproar that followed. "Laugh on!" he repeated with a swoop of his arm. "I don't care! Don't you care either, Mrs. Mount-Rhyswicke. Please sit where I can see your beautiful golden hair. Don't be afraid I'll kiss you again. I wouldn't do it for the whole world. You're one of the noblest women I ever knew. I feel that's true. I don't know how I know it, but I know it. Let 'em laugh!"

After this everything grew more and more hazy to him. For a time there was, in the centre of the haze, a nimbus of light which revealed his cards to him and the towers of chips which he constantly called for and which as constantly disappeared - like the towers of a castle in Spain. Then the haze thickened, and the one thing clear to him was a phrase from an old-time novel he had read long ago:

"Debt of honor."

The three words appeared to be written in flames against a background of dense fog. A debt of honor was as promissory note which had to be paid on Monday, and the appeal to the obdurate grandfather - a peer of England, the Earl of Mount-Rhyswicke, in fact - was made at midnight, Sunday. The fog grew still denser, lifted for a moment while he wrote his name many times on slips of blue paper; closed down once more, and again lifted - out-of-doors this time - to show him a lunatic ballet of moons dancing streakily upon the horizon.

He heard himself say quite clearly, "All right, old man,

thank you; but don't bother about me," to a pallid but humorous Cooley in evening clothes; the fog thickened; oblivion closed upon him for a seeming second....

VII.

THE NEXT MORNING

Suddenly he sat up in bed in his room at the Magnifique, gazing upon a disconsolate Cooley in gray tweeds who sat heaped in a chair at the foot of the bed with his head in his hands.

Mellin's first sensation was of utter mystification; his second was more corporeal: the consciousness of physical misery, of consuming fever, of aches that ran over his whole body, converging to a dreadful climax in his head, of a throat so immoderately partched it seemed to crackle, and a thirst so avid it was a passion. His eye fell upon a carafe of water on a chair at his bedside; he seized upon it with a shaking hand and drank half its contents before he set it down. The action attracted his companion's attention and he looked up, showing a pale and haggard countenance.

"How do you feel?" inquired Cooley with a wan smile.

Mellin's head dropped back upon the pillow and he made one or two painful efforts to speak before he succeeded in finding a ghastly semblance of his voice.

"I thought I was at Madame de Vaurigard's."

"You were," said the other, adding grimly: "We both were."

"But that was only a minute ago."

"It was six hours ago. It's goin' on ten o'clock in the morning."

"I don't understand how that can be. How did I get here?"

"I brought you. I was pretty bad, but you - I never saw anything like you! From the time you kissed Lady Mount-Rhyswicke -"

Mellin sat bolt upright in bed, staring wildly. He began to tremble violently.

"Don't you remember that?" asked Cooley.

Suddenly he did. The memory of it came with inexorable clarity, he crossed forearms over his horror-stricken face and fell back upon his pillow.

"Oh," he gasped. "Un-speakable! Un-speakable!"

"Lord! Don't worry about that! I don't think she minded."

"It's the thought of Madame de Vaurigard - it kills me! The horror of it - that I should do such a thing in her house! She'll never speak to me again, she oughtn't to; she ought to send her groom to beat me! You can't think what I've lost -"

"Can't I!" Mr. Cooley rose from his chair and began to

pace up and down the chamber. "I can guess to within a thousand francs of what *I've* lost! I had to get the hotel to cash a check on New York for me this morning. I've a habit of carrying all my money in bills, and a fool trick, too. Well, I'm cured of it!"

"Oh, if it were only a little *money* and nothing else that I'd lost! The money means nothing." Mellin choked.

"I suppose you're pretty well fixed. Well, so am I," Cooley shook his head, "but money certainly means something to me!"

"It wouldn't if you'd thrown away the most precious friendship of your life."

"See here," said Cooley, halting at the foot of the bed and looking at his stricken companion from beneath frowning brows, "I guess I can see how it is with you, and I'll tell you frankly it's been the same with me. I never met such a fascinating woman in my life: she throws a reg'ler ole-fashioned ~spell~ over you! Now I hate to say it, but I can't help it, because it plain hits me in the face every time I think of it; the truth is - well, sir, I'm afraid you and me have had little red soldier-coats and caps put on us and strings tied to our belts while we turned somersets for the children."

"I don't understand. I don't know what you're talking about."

"No? It seems to get more and more simple to me. I've been thinking it all over and over again. I can't ~help~ it! See here: I met Sneyd on the steamer, without any introduction. He sort of warmed into the game in the smoking-room, and he won straight along the trip. He called on me in London and took me to meet the Countess at her hotel. We three went to the theatre and lunch and so forth a few times; and when I left for Paris she turned up on the way: that's when you met her. Couple of days later, Sneyd came over, and he and the Countess introduced me to dear ole friend Pedlow. So you see, I don't rightly even know who any of 'em really *are*: just took 'em for granted, as it were. We had lots of fun, I admit that, honkin' about in my car. We only played cards once, and that was in her apartment the last night before I left Paris, but that one time Pedlow won fifteen thousand francs from me. When I told them my plans, how I was goin' to motor down to Rome, she said *she* would be in Rome - and, I tell you, I was happy as a poodle-pup about it. Sneyd said he might be in Rome along about then, and open-hearted ole Pedlow said not to be surprised if *he* turned up, too. Well, he did, almost to the minute, and in the meantime she'd got *you* hooked on, fine and tight."

"I don't understand you," Mellin lifted himself painfully on an elbow. "I don't know what you're getting at, but it seems to me that you're speaking disrespectfully of an angel that I've insulted, and I -"

"Now see here, Mellin, I'll tell you something." The boy's white face showed sudden color and there was a catch in his voice. "I was - I've been mighty near in *love* with that woman! But I've had a kind of a shock; I've got my common-sense back, and I'm ~not~, any more. I don't know exactly how much money I had, but it was between thirty-five and thirty-eight thousand francs, and Sneyd won it all after we took off the limit - over seven thousand dollars - at her table last night. Putting two and two together, honestly it looks bad. It looks *mighty* bad! Now, I'm pretty well fixed, and yesterday I didn't care whether school kept or not, but seven thousand dollars is real money to anybody! My old man worked pretty hard for his first seven thousand, I guess, and" - he gulped - "he'd think a lot of me for lettin' go of it the way I did last night, *wouldn't* he? You never *see* things like this till the next morning! And you remember that other woman sat where she could see every hand *you* drew, and the Countess -"

"Stop!" Mellin flung one arm up violently, striking the headboard with his knuckles. "I won't hear a syllable against Madame de Vaurigard!" Young Cooley regarded him steadily for a moment. "Have you remembered yet," he said slowly, "how much *you* lost last night?"

"I only remember that I behaved like an unspeakable boor in the presence of the divinest creature that ever -"

Cooley disregarded the outburst, and said:

"When we settled, you had a pad of express company checks worth six hundred dollars. You signed all of 'em and turned 'em over to Sneyd with three one-hundred-lire bills, which was all the cash you had with you. Then you gave him your note for twelve thousand francs to be paid within three days. You made a great deal of fuss about its being a 'debt of honor.'" He paused. "You hadn't remembered that, had you?"

Mellin had closed his eyes. He lay quite still and made no answer.

"No, I'll bet you hadn't," said Cooley, correctly

deducing the fact. "You're well off, or you wouldn't be at this hotel, and, for all I know, you may be fixed so you won't mind your loss as much as I do mine; but it ought to make you kind of charitable toward my suspicions of Madame de Vaurigard's friends."

The six hundred dollars in express company checks and the three hundred-lire bills were all the money the unhappy Mellin had in the world, and until he could return to Cranston and go back to work in the real-estate office again, he had no prospect of any more. He had not even his steamer ticket. In the shock of horror and despair he whispered brokenly:

"I don't care if they 're the worst people in the world, they're better than I am!"

The other's gloom cleared a little at this. "Well, you *have* got it!" he exclaimed briskly. "You don't know how different you'll feel after a long walk in the open air." He looked at his watch. "I've got to go and see what that newspaper-man, Cornish, wants; it's ten o'clock. I'll be back after a while; I want to reason this out with you. I don't deny but it's possible I'm wrong; anyway, you think it over while I'm gone. You take a good hard think, will you?"

As he closed the door, Mellin slowly drew the coverlet over his head. It was as if he covered the face of some one who had just died.

VIII.

WHAT CORNISH KNEW

Two hours passed before young Cooley returned. He knocked twice without a reply; then he came in.

The coverlet was still over Mellin's head.

"Asleep?" asked Cooley.

"No."

The coverlet was removed by a shaking hand.

"Murder!" exclaimed Cooley sympathetically, at sight of the other's face. "A night off certainly does things to you! Better let me get you some -"

"No. I'll be all right - after while."

"Then I'll go right ahead with our little troubles. I've decided to leave for Paris by the one-thirty and haven't got a whole lot of time. Cornish is here with me in the hall: he's got something to say that's important for you to hear, and I'm goin' to bring him right in." He waved his hand toward the door, which he had left open. "Come along, Cornish. Poor ole Mellin'll play Du Barry with us and give us a morning leevy while he listens in a bed with a palanquin to it. Now let's draw up chairs and be sociable."

The journalist came in, smoking a long cigar, and took the chair the youth pushed toward him; but, after a twinkling glance through his big spectacles at the face on the pillow, he rose and threw the cigar out of the window.

"Go ahead," said Cooley. "I want you to tell him just what you told me, and when you're through I want to see if he doesn't think I'm Sherlock Holmes' little brother."

"If Mr. Mellin does not feel too ill," said Cornish dryly; "I know how painful such cases sometimes -"

"No." Mellin moistened his parched lips and made a pitiful effort to smile. "I'll be all right very soon."

"I am very sorry," began the journalist, "that I wasn't able to get a few words with Mr. Cooley yesterday evening. Perhaps you noticed that I tried as hard as I could, without using actual force" - he laughed - "to detain him."

"You did your best," agreed Cooley ruefully, "and I did my worst. Nobody ever listens till the next day!"

"Well, I'm glad no vital damage was done, anyway," said Cornish. "It would have been pretty hard lines if you two young fellows had been poor men, but as it is you're probably none the worse for a lesson like this."

"You seem to think seven thousand dollars is a joke," remarked Cooley.

Cornish laughed again. "You see, it flatters me to think my time was so valuable that a ten minutes' talk with me would have saved so much money."

"I doubt it," said Cooley. "Ten to one we'd neither of us have believed you - last night!"

"I doubt it, too." Cornish turned to Mellin. "I hear that you, Mr. Mellin, are still of the opinion that you were dealing with straight people?"

Mellin managed to whisper "Yes."

"Then," said Cornish, "I'd better tell you just what I know about it, and you can form your own opinion as to whether I do know or not. I have been in the newspaper business on this side for fifteen years, and my headquarters are in Paris, where these people are very well known. The man who calls himself 'Chandler Pedlow' was a faro-dealer for Tom Stout in Chicago when Stout's place was broken up, a good many years ago. There was a real Chandler Pedlow in Congress from a California district in the early nineties, but he is dead. This man's name is Ben Welch: he's a professional swindler; and the Englishman, Sneyd, is another; a quiet man, not so well known as Welch, and not nearly so clever, but a good 'feeder' for him. The very attractive Frenchwoman who calls herself 'Comtesse de Vaurigard' is generally believed to be Sneyd's wife, though I could not take the stand on that myself. Welch is the brains of the organization: you mightn't think it, but he's a very brilliant man - he might have made a great reputation in business if he'd been straight - and, with this woman's help, he's carried out some really astonishing schemes. His manner is clumsy; *he* knows that, bless you, but it's the only manner he can manage, and she is so adroit she can sugar-coat even such a pill as that and coax people to swallow it. I don't know anything about the Italian who is working with them down here. But a gang of the Welch-Vaurigard-Sneyd type has tentacles all over the Continent; such people are in touch with sharpers everywhere, you see."

"Yes," Cooley interpolated, "and with woolly little lambkins, too."

"Well," chuckled Cornish, "that's the way they make their living, you know."

"Go on and tell him the rest of it," urged Cooley.

"About Lady Mount-Rhyswicke," said Cornish, "it seems strange enough, but she has a perfect right to her name. She is a good deal older than she looks, and I've heard she used to be remarkably beautiful. Her third husband was Lord George Mount-Rhyswicke, a man who'd been dropped from his clubs, and he deserted her in 1903, but she has not divorced him. It is said that he is somewhere in South America; however, as to that I do not know."

Mr. Cornish put the very slightest possible emphasis on the word "know," and proceeded:

"I've heard that she is sincerely attached to him and sends him money from time to time, when she has it - though that, too, is third-hand information. She has been *declasse* ever since her first divorce. That was a 'celebrated case,' and she's dropped down pretty far in the world, though I judge she's a good deal the best of this crowd. Exactly what her relations to the others are

I don't know, but I imagine that she's pretty thick with 'em."

"Just a little!" exclaimed Cooley. "She sits behind one of the lambkins and Helene behind the other while they get their woolly wool clipped. I suppose the two of 'em signaled what was in every hand we held, though I'm sure they needn't have gone to the trouble! Fact is, I don't see why they bothered about goin' through the form of playin' cards with us at all. They could have taken it away without that! Whee!" Mr. Cooley whistled loud and long. "And there's loads of wise young men on the ocean now, hurryin' over to take our places in the pens. Well, they can have *mine*! Funny, Mellin: nobody would come up to you or me in the Grand Central in New York and try to sell us greenbacks just as good as real. But we come over to Europe with our pockets full o' money and start in to see the Big City with Jesse James in a false mustache on one arm, and Lucresha Borgy, under an assumed name, on the other!"

"I am afraid I agree with you," said Cornish; "though I must say that, from all I hear, Madame de Vaurigard might put an atmosphere about a thing which would deceive almost any one who wasn't on his guard. When a Parisienne of her sort is clever at all she's irresistible."

"I believe you," Cooley sighed deeply.

"Yesterday evening, Mr. Mellin," continued the journalist, "when I saw the son of my old friend in company with Welch and Sneyd, of course I tried to warn him. I've often seen them in Paris, though I believe they have no knowledge of me. As I've said, they are notorious, especially Welch, yet they have managed, so far, to avoid any difficulty with the Paris police, and, I'm sorry to say, it might be hard to actually prove anything against them. You couldn't *prove* that anything was crooked last night, for instance. For that matter, I don't suppose you want to. Mr. Cooley wishes to accept his loss and bear it, and I take it that that will be your attitude, too. In regard to the note you gave Sneyd, I hope you will refuse to pay; I don't think that they would dare press the matter."

"Neither do I," Mr. Cooley agreed. "I left a silver cigarette-case at the apartment last night, and after talkin' to Cornish a while ago, I sent my man for it with a note to her that'll make 'em all sit up and take some notice. The gang's all there together, you can be sure. I asked for Sneyd and Pedlow in the office and found they'd gone out early this morning leavin' word they wouldn't be back till midnight. And, see here; I know I'm easy, but somehow I believe you're even a softer piece o' meat than I am. I want you to promise me that whatever happens you won't pay that I O U."

Mellin moistened his lips in vain. He could not answer.

"I want you to promise me not to pay it," repeated Cooley earnestly.

"I promise," gasped Mellin.

"You won't pay it no matter what they do?"

"No."

This seemed to reassure Mr. Cooley.

"Well," he said, "I've got to hustle to get my car shipped and make the train. Cornish has finished his job down here and he's goin' with me. I want to get out. The whole thing's left a mighty bad taste in my mouth, and I'd go crazy if I didn't get away from it. Why don't you jump into your clothes and come along, too?"

"I can't."

"Well," said the young man with a sympathetic shake of the head, "you certainly look sick. It may be better if you stay in bed till evening: a train's a mighty mean place for the day after. But I wouldn't hang around here too long. If you want money, all you have to do is to ask the hotel to cash a check on your home bank; they're always glad to do that for Americans." He turned to the door. "Mr. Cornish, if you're goin' to help me about shipping the car, I'm ready."

"So am I. Good-by, Mr. Mellin."

"Good-by," Mellin said feebly - "and thank you."

Young Cooley came back to the bedside and shook the other's feverish hand. "Good-by, ole man. I'm awful sorry it's all happened, but I'm glad it didn't cost you quite as much money as it did me. Otherwise I expect it's hit us about equally hard. I wish - I wish I could find a *inice one*" - the youth gulped over something not unlike a sob - "as fascinatin' as her!"

Most people have had dreams of approaching dangers in the path of which their bodies remained inert; when, in spite of the frantic wish to fly, it was impossible to move, while all the time the horror crept closer and closer. This was Mellin's state as he saw the young man going. It was absolutely necessary to ask Cooley for help, to beg him for a loan. But he could not.

He saw Cooley's hand on the doorknob; saw the door swing open.

"Good-by, again," Cooley said; "and good luck to you!"

Mellin's will strove desperately with the shame that held him silent.

The door was closing.

"Oh, Cooley," called Mellin hoarsely.

"Yes. What?"

"J-j-just good-by," said Mellin.

And with that young Cooley was gone.

IX.

EXPIATION

A multitudinous clangor of bells and a dozen neighboring chimes rang noon; then the rectangular oblongs of hot sunlight that fell from the windows upon the carpet of Mellin's room began imperceptibly to shift their angles and move eastward. From the stone pavement of the street below came the sound of horses pawing and the voices of waiting cabmen; then bells again, and more bells; clamoring the slow and cruel afternoon into the past. But all was silent in Mellin's room, save when, from time to time, a long, shuddering sigh came from the bed.

The unhappy young man had again drawn the coverlet over his head, but not to sleep: it was more like a forlorn and desperate effort to hide, as if he crept into a hole, seeking darkness to cover the shame and fear that racked his soul. For though his shame had been too great to let him confess to young Cooley and ask for help, his fear was as great as his shame; and it increased as the hours passed. In truth his case was desperate. Except the people who had stripped him, Cooley was the only person in all of Europe with whom he had more than a very casual acquaintance. At home, in Cranston, he had no friends susceptible to such an appeal as it was vitally necessary for him to make. His relatives were not numerous: there were two aunts, the widows of his father's brothers, and a number of old-maid cousins; and he had an uncle in Iowa, a country minister whom he had not seen for years. But he could not cable to any of these for money; nor could he quite conjure his imagination into picturing any of them sending it if he did. And even to cable he would have to pawn his watch, which was an old-fashioned one of silver and might not bring enough to pay the charges.

He began to be haunted by fragmentary, prophetic visions - confused but realistic in detail, and horridly probable - of his ejectment from the hotel, perhaps arrest and trial. He wondered what they did in Italy to people who "beat" hotels; and, remembering what some one had told him of the dreadfulness of Italian jails, convulsive shudderings seized upon him.

The ruddy oblongs of sunlight crawled nearer to the east wall of the room, stretching themselves thinner and thinner, until finally they were not there at all, and the room was left in deepening grayness. Carriages, one after the other, in unintermittent succession, rumbled up to the hotel-entrance beneath the window, bringing goldfish for the Pincio and the fountains of Villa Borghese. Wild strains from the Hungarian orchestra, rhapsodical twankings of violins, and the runaway arpeggios of a zither crazed with speed-mania, skipped along the corridors and lightly through Mellin's door. In his mind's eye he saw the gay crowd in the watery light, the little tables where only five days ago he had sat with the loveliest of all the anemone-like ladies....

The beautifully-dressed tea-drinkers were there now,

under the green glass dome, prattling and smiling, those people he had called his own. And as the music sounded louder, faster, wilder and wilder with the gipsy madness - then in that darkening bedchamber his soul became articulate in a cry of humiliation

"God in His mercy forgive me, how raw I was!"

A vision came before his closed eyes; the maple-bordered street in Cranston, the long, straight, wide street where Mary Kramer lived; a summer twilight; Mary in her white muslin dress on the veranda steps, and a wistaria vine climbing the post beside her, half-embowering her. How cool and sweet and good she looked! How dear - and how ~kind~! - she had always been to him.

Dusk stole through the windows: the music ceased and the tea-hour was over. The carriages were departing, bearing the gay people who went away laughing, calling last words to one another, and, naturally, quite unaware that a young man, who, five days before, had adopted them and called them "his own," was lying in a darkened room above them, and crying like a child upon his pillow.

X.

THE CAB AT THE CORNER

A ten o'clock, a page bearing a card upon a silver tray knocked upon the door, and stared with wide-eyed astonishment at the disordered gentleman who opened it.

The card was Lady Mount-Rhyswicke's. Underneath the name was written:

If you are there will you give me a few minutes? I am waiting in a cab at the next corner by the fountain.

Mellin's hand shook as he read. He did not doubt that she came as an emissary; probably they meant to hound him for payment of the note he had given Sneyd, and at that thought he could have shrieked with hysterical laughter.

"Do you speak English?" he asked.

"Spik little. Yes."

"Who gave you this card?"

"Coachman," said the boy. "He wait risposta."

"Tell him to say that I shall be there in five minutes."

"Fi' minute. Yes. Good-by."

Mellin was partly dressed - he had risen half an hour earlier and had been distractedly pacing the floor when the page knocked - and he completed his toilet quickly. He passed down the corridors, descended by the stairway (feeling that to use the elevator would be another abuse of the confidence of the hotel company) and slunk across the lobby with the look and the sensations of a tramp who knows that he will be kicked into the street if anybody catches sight of him.

A closed cab stood near the fountain at the next corner. There was a trunk on the box by the driver, and the roof was piled with bags and rugs. He approached uncertainly.

"Is - is this - is it Lady Mount-Rhyswicke?" he stammered pitifully.

She opened the door.

"Yes. Will you get in? We'll just drive round the block if you don't mind. I'll bring you back here in ten minutes." And when he had tremulously complied, "*Avanti, cocchiere*," she called to the driver, and the tired little cab-horse began to draw them slowly along the deserted street.

Lady Mount-Rhyswicke maintained silence for a time, while her companion waited, his heart pounding with dreadful apprehensions. Finally she gave a short, hard laugh and said:

"I saw your face by the corner light. Been havin' a hard day of it?"

The fear of breaking down kept him from answering. He gulped painfully once or twice, and turned his face away from her. Light enough from a streetlamp shone in for her to see.

"I was rather afraid you'd refuse," she said seriously. "Really, I wonder you were willin' to come!"

"I was - I was afraid not to." He choked out the confession with the recklessness of final despair.

"So?" she said, with another short laugh. Then she resumed her even, tired monotone: "Your little friend Cooley's note this morning gave us all a rather fair notion as to what you must be thinkin' of us. He seems to have found a sort of walkin' 'Who's-Who-on-the-Continent' since last night. Pity for some people he didn't find it before! I don't think I'm sympathetic with your little Cooley. I 'guess,' as you Yankees say, 'he can stand it.' But" - her voice suddenly became louder - "I'm not in the business of robbin' babies and orphans, no, my dear friends, nor of helpin' anybody else to rob them either! - Here you are!"

She thrust into his hand a small packet, securely wrapped in paper and fastened with rubber bands. "There's your block of express checks for six hundred dollars and your I 0 U to Sneyd with it. Take better care of it next time."

He had been tremulous enough, but at that his whole body began to shake violently.

"*What!*" he quavered.

"I say, take better care of it next time," she said, dropping again into her monotone. "I didn't have such an easy time gettin' it back from them as you might think. I've got rather a sore wrist, in fact."

She paused at an inarticulate sound from him.

"Oh, that's soon mended," she laughed drearily. "The truth is, it's been a good thing for me - your turning up. They're gettin' in too deep water for me, Helene and her friends, and I've broken with the lot, or they've broken with me, whichever it is. We couldn't hang together after the fightin' we've done to-day. I had to do a lot of threatenin' and things. Welch was ugly, so I had to be ugly too. Never mind" - she checked an uncertain effort of his to speak - "I saw what you were like, soon as we sat down at the table last night - how new you were and all that. It needed only a glance to see that Helene had made a mistake about you. She'd got a notion you were a millionaire like the little Cooley, but I knew better from your talk. She's clever, but she's French, and she can't get it out of her head that you could be an American and not a millionaire. Of course, they *all* knew better when you brought out your express checks and talked like somebody in one of the old-time story-books about 'debts of honor.' Even Helene understood then that the express checks were all you had." She laughed. "I didn't have any trouble gettin' the *note* back!"

She paused again for a moment, then resumed: "There isn't much use our goin' over it all, but I want you to know one thing. Your little friend Cooley made it rather clear that he accused Helene and me of signalin'.

Well, I didn't. Perhaps that's the reason you didn't lose as much as he did; I can't say. And one thing more: all this isn't goin' to do you any harm. I'm not very keen about philosophy and religion and that, but I believe if you're let in for a lot of trouble, and it only *half* kills you, you can get some good of it."

"Do you think," he stammered - "do you think I'm worth saving?"

She smiled faintly and said:

"You've probably got a sweetheart in the States somewhere - a nice girl, a pretty young thing who goes to church and thinks you're a great man, perhaps? Is it so?"

"I am not worthy," he began, choked suddenly, then finished - "to breathe the same air!"

"That's quite right," Lady Mount-Rhyswicke assured him. "Think what you'd think of her if she'd got herself into the same sort of scrape by doin' the things you've been doin'! And remember *that* if you ever feel impatient with her, or have any temptations to superiority in times to come. And yet" - for the moment she spoke earnestly - "you go back to your little girl, but don't you tell her a word of this. You couldn't even tell her that meetin' you has helped me, because she wouldn't understand."

"Nor do I. I can't."

"Oh, it's simple. I saw that if I was gettin' down to where I was robbin' babies and orphans...." The cab halted. "Here's your corner. I told him only to go round the block and come back. Good-by. I'm off for Amalfi. It's a good place to rest."

He got out dazedly, and the driver cracked his whip over the little horse; but Mellin lifted a detaining hand.

"*A spet*," called Lady Mount-Rhyswicke to the driver. "What is it, Mr. Mellin?"

"I can't - I can't look you in the face," he stammered, his attitude perfectly corroborative of his words. "I would - oh, I would kneel in the dust here before you -"

"Some of the poetry you told me you write?"

"I've never written any poetry," he said, not looking up. "Perhaps I can - now. What I want to say is - I'm so ashamed of it - I don't know how to get the words out, but I must. I may never see you again, and I must. I 'm sorry - please try to forgive me - I wasn't myself when I did it -"

"Blurt it out; that's the best way."

"I'm sorry," he floundered - "I'm sorry I kissed you."

She laughed her tired laugh and said in her tired voice the last words he was ever destined to hear from her:

"Oh, I don't mind, if you don't. It was so innocent, it was what decided me."

One of the hundreds of good saints that belong to Rome must have overheard her and pitied the young man, for it is ascribable only to some such special act of mercy that Mellin understood (and he did) exactly what she meant.

Choose from Thousands of 1stWorldLibrary Classics By

Adolphus William Ward
Aesop
Agatha Christie
Alexander Aaronsohn
Alexander Kielland
Alexandre Dumas
Alfred Gatty
Alfred Ollivant
Alice Duer Miller
Alice Turner Curtis
Alice Dunbar
Ambrose Bierce
Amelia E. Barr
Andrew Lang
Andrew McFarland Davis
Anna Sewell
Annie Besant
Annie Hamilton Donnell
Annie Payson Call
Anton Chekhov
Arnold Bennett
Arthur Conan Doyle
Arthur Ransome
Atticus
B. M. Bower
Basil King
Bayard Taylor
Ben Macomber
Booth Tarkington
Bram Stoker
C. Collodi
C. E. Orr
C. M. Ingleby
Carolyn Wells
Catherine Parr Traill
Charles A. Eastman
Charles Dickens
Charles Dudley Warner
Charles Farrar Browne
Charles Ives
Charles Kingsley
Charles Lathrop Pack
Charles Whibley
Charles Willing Beale
Charlotte M. Braeme
Charlotte M.Yonge
Clair W. Hayes
Clarence Day Jr.
Clarence E. Mulford

Clemence Housman
Confucius
Cornelis DeWitt Wilcox
Cyril Burleigh
D. H. Lawrence
Daniel Defoe
David Garnett
Don Carlos Janes
Donald Keyhole
Dorothy Kilner
Dougan Clark
E. Nesbit
E.P.Roe
E. Phillips Oppenheim
Edgar Allan Poe
Edgar Rice Burroughs
Edith Wharton
Edward J. O'Biren
John Cournos
Edwin L. Arnold
Eleanor Atkins
Elizabeth Cleghorn
Gaskell
Elizabeth Von Arnim
Ellem Key
Emily Dickinson
Erasmus W. Jones
Ernie Howard Pie
Ethel Turner
Ethel Watts Mumford
Eugenie Foa
Eugene Wood
Evelyn Everett-Green
Everard Cotes
F. J. Cross
Federick Austin Ogg
Ferdinand Ossendowski
Francis Bacon
Francis Darwin
Frances Hodgson Burnett
Frank Gee Patchin
Frank Harris
Frank Jewett Mather
Frank L. Packard
Frederick Trevor Hill
Frederick Winslow Taylor
Friedrich Kerst
Friedrich Nietzsche
Fyodor Dostoyevsky

Gabrielle E. Jackson
Garrett P. Serviss
Gaston Leroux
George Ade
Geroge Bernard Shaw
George Ebers
George Eliot
George MacDonald
George Orwell
George Tucker
George W. Cable
George Wharton James
Gertrude Atherton
Grace E. King
Grant Allen
Guillermo A. Sherwell
Gulielma Zollinger
Gustav Flaubert
H. A. Cody
H. B. Irving
H. G. Wells
H. H. Munro
H. Irving Hancock
H. Rider Haggard
H. W. C. Davis
Hamilton Wright Mabie
Hans Christian Andersen
Harold Avery
Harold McGrath
Harriet Beecher Stowe
Harry Houidini
Helent Hunt Jackson
Helen Nicolay
Hendy David Thoreau
Henrik Ibsen
Henry Adams
Henry Ford
Henry Frost
Henry James
Henry Jones Ford
Henry Seton Merriman
Henry Wadsworth
Longfellow
Henry W Longfellow
Herbert A. Giles
Herbert N. Casson
Herman Hesse
Homer
Honore De Balzac

Horace Walpole
Horatio Alger, Jr.
Howard Pyle
Howard R. Garis
Hugh Lofting
Hugh Walpole
Humphry Ward
Ian Maclaren
Israel Abrahams
J.G.Austin
J. Henri Fabre
J. M. Barrie
J. Macdonald Oxley
J. S. Knowles
J. Storer Clouston
Jack London
Jacob Abbott
James Allen
James Lane Allen
James Andrews
James Baldwin
James DeMille
James Joyce
James Oliver Curwood
James Oppenheim
James Otis
Jane Austen
Jens Peter Jacobsen
Jerome K. Jerome
John Burroughs
John F. Kennedy
John Gay
John Glasworthy
John Habberton
John Joy Bell
John Milton
John Philip Sousa
Jonathan Swift
Joseph Carey
Joseph Conrad
Joseph Jacobs
Julian Hawthrone
Julies Vernes
Justin Huntly McCarthy
Kakuzo Okakura
Kenneth Grahame
Kate Langley Bosher
L. A. Abbot
L. T. Meade
L. Frank Baum
Laura Lee Hope

Laurence Housman
Leo Tolstoy
Leonid Andreyev
Lewis Carroll
Lilian Bell
Lloyd Osbourne
Louis Tracy
Louisa May Alcott
Lucy Fitch Perkins
Lucy Maud Montgomery
Lydia Miller Middleton
Lyndon Orr
M. H. Adams
Margaret E. Sangster
Margaret Vandercook
Maria Edgeworth
Maria Thompson Daviess
Mariano Azuela
Marion Polk Angellotti
Mark Overton
Mark Twain
Mary Austin
Mary Cole
Mary Rowlandson
Mary Wollstonecraft
Shelley
Max Beerbohm
Myra Kelly
Nathaniel Hawthrone
O. F. Walton
Oscar Wilde
Owen Johnson
P.G.Wodehouse
Paul and Mable Thorn
Paul G. Tomlinson
Paul Severing
Peter B. Kyne
Plato
R. Derby Holmes
R. L. Stevenson
Rabindranath Tagore
Rahul Alvares
Ralph Waldo Emmerson
Rene Descartes
Rex E. Beach
Richard Harding Davis
Richard Jefferies
Robert Barr
Robert Frost
Robert Gordon Anderson
Robert L. Drake

Robert Lansing
Robert Michael Ballantyne
Robert W. Chambers
Rosa Nouchette Carey
Ross Kay
Rudyard Kipling
Samuel B. Allison
Samuel Hopkins Adams
Sarah Bernhardt
Selma Lagerlof
Sherwood Anderson
Sigmund Freud
Standish O'Grady
Stanley Weyman
Stella Benson
Stephen Crane
Stewart Edward White
Stijn Streuvels
Swami Abhedananda
Swami Parmananda
T. S. Ackland
The Princess Der Ling
Thomas A. Janvier
Thomas A Kempis
Thomas Anderton
Thomas Bailey Aldrich
Thomas Bulfinch
Thomas De Quincey
Thomas H. Huxley
Thomas Hardy
Thomas More
Thornton W. Burgess
U. S. Grant
Valentine Williams
Victor Appleton
Virginia Woolf
Walter Scott
Washington Irving
Wilbur Lawton
Wilkie Collins
Willa Cather
Willard F. Baker
William Makepeace
Thackeray
William W. Walter
Winston Churchill
Yei Theodora Ozaki
Young E. Allison
Zane Grey

www.ingramcontent.com/pod-product-compliance
Lightning Source LLC
Chambersburg PA
CBHW032026040426
42448CB00006B/732